Travelers in an

Antique Land

Travelers in an Antique Land

poems by

WILLIAM STUDEBAKER

photographs by

RUSSELL HEPWORTH

University of Idaho Press   MOSCOW, IDAHO

1997

Copyright © 1997 by the University of Idaho Press

Published by the University of Idaho Press, Moscow, Idaho 83844-1107

Design by Caroline Hagen

Printed in Hong Kong

01   00   99   98   97   5   4   3   2   1

Library of Congress Cataloging-in-Publication Data

Studebaker, William.
Travelers in an antique land / poems by William Studebaker : photographs by Russell Hepworth.
p.   cm.
ISBN 0-89301-203-3 (alk. paper)
1. West (U.S.)—Poetry.   I. Hepworth, Russell, 1949–   . II. Title.
PS3569.T84T73   1997
811'.54—dc20   96-38996
CIP

OZYMANDIAS

I met a traveler from an antique land

Who said: Two vast and trunkless legs of stone

Stand in the desert . . . Near them, on the sand,

Half sunk, a shattered visage lies, whose frown,

And wrinkled lip, and sneer of cold command,

Tell that its sculptor well those passions read

Which yet survive, stamped on these lifeless things,

The hand that mocked them, and the heart that fed;

And on the pedestal these words appear:

"My name is Ozymandias, king of kings;

Look on my works, ye Mighty, and despair!"

Nothing beside remains. Round the decay

Of that colossal wreck, boundless and bare

The lone and level sands stretch far away.

—PERCY BYSSHE SHELLEY

Contents

Acknowledgments

Some of these poems have been previously published in *Boise Magazine* ("The Big Sky Map of Idaho"); *cold-drill* ("Terra Incognito" and "The Skies Over Nevada"); *The Dickinson Review* ("Butte City, Idaho National Energy Laboratory, Acceleration, Half Lives"); *Greenfield Review* ("Nightfire"); *High Country News* ("Looking for the Perfect Landscape"); *Idaho Mountain Express* ("Hiking Out of a Proposed Wilderness Area" and "Honeymoon" now "Honeymoon in Owyhee"); *Limberlost Review* ("Directions to Wilson Butte"); *New Mexico Humanities Review* ("Drinking From a Cattle Trough"); *Out Post Magazine* ("Walking the High Desert in Winter"); *The Red Neck Review* ("The Booming Ground" now "Instructions for a Ceremony in April"); *Seattle Times* ("North of Bliss"); *Slackwater Review* ("The Wind's Ecclesiastical History of Utah" and "Jukebox Cave").

"The Bruneau Desert," "Cathedral Rock," and "Wintered on the North Fork" appeared in *Everything Goes Without Saying* (Confluence Press, 1978).

"Basco" appeared in *Eight Idaho Poets* (University of Idaho Press, 1979).

"The Space Closest to Our Bodies," "Collecting Camas," "In Hells Canyon," "Abandoning the Body," and "Thousand Springs, Idaho: Outlet for Lost Rivers" were published in *Trailing the Raven* (Limberlost Press, 1982).

"For Your Part" was published in the Limberlost Press Postcard Series (Limberlost Press, 1987).

"Trace Elements Around the Saylor Creek Bombing Range" appeared in the anthology *A Gathering of Poets* (Kent State University Press, 1992).

"City of Rocks" was read on the television program *Outdoor Idaho* (1994).

All definitions adapted and reproduced by permission from *The American Heritage Dictionary of the English Language*. Copyright © 1981 by Houghton Mifflin Company.

The poem "Ozymandias" is quoted as printed in the *Collected Works of Percy Bysshe Shelley*.

We thank the following galleries for exhibiting poems and photographs. "Desert Passage" series: The Sunspot (College of Southern Idaho) and The Mind's Eye (Idaho State University).

Bill thanks Judy with whom he has been honeymooning for 28 years; his children Tona, Robert, Tyler, and Eric who have eaten much dust; and his parents Bob and Betty Studebaker who insisted that he "play outside."

Russ thanks Harriet Hepworth for a first camera, film, and endless encouragement; and Rayford Hepworth for a love and respect of the land that lives on; and Anne for making the desert passage.

Desert

des·ert[1] (dĕz´ərt) *n.* A region rendered barren or partially barren by environmental extremes, especially by low rainfall. —*adj.* Of, pertaining to, or characteristic of a desert: barren and uninhabited: desolate: *a desert island.* [Middle English, from Old French, from Late Latin *dēsertum*, from Latin, neuter past participle of *dēserere,* to abandon. DESERT.]

Passage

pas·sage (păs´ĭj) *n. Abbr.* **pass. 1.** The act or process of passing: **a.** A movement from one place to another: a going by, through, over, or across: transit. **b.** The process of elapsing. **c.** The process of passing from one state, condition, or stage to another: transition. **d.** *Obsolete.* Death. **e.** The enactment into law of a legislative measure. **2.** A journey, especially one by air or water. **3. a.** The right to travel on something, especially a ship: *to book a passage.* **b.** The price paid for this. **4.** The right, permission, or power to come and go freely. **5. a.** A path, channel, or duct through, over, or along which something may pass: *the nasal passages.* **b.** A corridor. **6.** An occurrence between two persons: **a.** An exchange of words, arguments, or vows. **b.** An exchange of blows: *passage at arms.* **7.** A segment of a literary work: *a celebrated passage from Gibbon.* **8.** *Music.* A segment of a composition. **9.** *Medicine.* An emptying of the bowels. —See Synonyms at **way.** [Middle English, from Old French, from *passer,* to PASS.]

THE SPACE CLOSEST TO OUR BODIES

Imagine some tan grass and sage,
monoliths and blow outs,
flatness the feet cannot believe,
distance the eye laughs at
as it fumbles blindly
with the ends of all time.

Imagine everything here moves
(even the cactus will come close
to a sleeping man
and the beetle will tunnel
under the arch of his foot)
and a full half-moon
is enough light for gray things.

Here our secret voice is too loud.
When we think, the desert hushes . . .
so quiet jack rabbits can hear
owls listening with one ear . . .
so quiet when a vulture beckons
with the bones of our hand
our shadow makes a dragging sound
like dry skin over rock.

Inside our selves, there is nothing
anyone can say to us.
We learn to hear a voice
with no sound, with no tongue
with no mouth, as if the air
itself was a way of speaking.
We have become easily startled
because we are living
in the space closest to our bodies.

HIKING OUT AT EVENING FROM A PROPOSED WILDERNESS AREA

Where the trail bends back toward
what we have just climbed
we sit like coyotes
uncertain of what we see—
our ears pointed
in different directions.

What we expect to come
comes in some other way
than that which we watch.
Our eyes make adjustments:
the pupils relax
the retinas shift capacities—
drawing exact distinctions out of gray.

(Each of us huddles
closer to a fire we left behind.
We are already beginning to feel
for solitude—a fragile memory
we have sworn to preserve.)

And now on the last leg of our journey,
we step over shadows skittering free
in the darkening desert
leaving tracks where we stood
but could not stand still.

CATHEDRAL ROCK

Plants still lean for the sun
and roots find a way—and dreams.

The smallest drop of water ebbs
though its roots never let go

like blue following the sun down
through a green slit.

Explode, wave, and . . .

prayer fans settle over
the nest of the sun.

Someone calls it darkness
and lights a lantern of sand.

WALKING THE HIGH DESERT IN WINTER

Come over this hill and you are in snow
    country.
Here the desert rises to its own height:
in winter high enough for snow
in summer too low for rain.

This is a place you can't memorize.
Here it is easiest to think with the eyes
    closed.
The landscape is like a piece of your mind
you never visit, and to see it
you must bring the light of desire
and go on until you find a way
through the dark side of yourself.

Your hands can cup the cold air
and bring it close to your chin.
Your eyes can pull the hawk out of the sky.
Your breath can dance on the frozen snakes
or you can translate your voice into wind.

This is a place without appointment.
No one expects you today or tomorrow.
(Even the bees, asleep in God's Pocket,
keep no schedule.)

The horizon swings open
like a shadow hinged
to its own reflection
to a place deep inside of you—
half dark, half light.
This is real only to experience.

And your breath, a small map
of where you're going,
puffs out ahead of you.

THE BRUNEAU DESERT

This is where God spent a day
rough-framing the canyons,
troweling the flats.
Said He'd be back.
Hasn't been, except at night.
I hear Him then, settling down
in the King's Chair:
the canyons fill with sound
only the wind can make;
owls limp their way
through the darkness;
the smallest rock
holds its breath;
sand dunes freeze.

There is something
God loves here:
things still inside the earth
cliffs full of figures . . .
a place where even He can brood.

On nights like this
we all wait.
His hand could come, anytime.

Occasionally a finger
ran out to a point
no one would defend

and the land, held up
after a long trial
for being too flat,

was sentenced
to stand on edge
to make a wall of itself

only birds could climb.

On the rim an artist
set up an easel

drawing out the sentence
giving some canyons
solitary for life.

Others, a single stroke
expedited
a brush with the law.

Now in the gallery
the artist's work hangs—
still—the only record

of silence being executed.

NORTH OF BLISS

Rock, sage, cheatgrass, and sunflowers
a half-dozen canyons
magpies, hawks, and horned larks
a thin stream
that everything comes down to
eventually
and wind that talks a mile a minute
and snakes that rattle
like the inside of your head
filling with sand
and dinosaurs that sleep beneath the hill
(their backs arched against the ridge)
and things that grow so even . . .
(the grass, short as beard stubble,
pierces the sky
without lifting a blade)
and stones that lie among themselves
   snoring—
too young to open their eyes.

AROUND THE JARBIDGE

Out here water is all english
making odd shots off canyon walls
falling into pockets
the bottom's out of.
You have to wait for weather—
the kind you want—all day, all year.

And the bank
that curb on the edge of the world
isn't faithful. It turns on you:
all cliff and boulders,
snakes that strike
leaving hexes in the sand.
(If you're going to be bitten
it's best to cut your leg off first.)

And in the winter
the high desert holds out
against itself: seeps stop.
Juniper and sage twist.
Coyote and grouse play Starvation.
Rattlers rewind.
And owls bark at the hush
of night slipping on ice.

LOOKING FOR THE PERFECT LANDSCAPE

An angus, tits up to the sun
lies bloated in the barrow pit.

Below the berm coyote bounces
after a mouse and gives me
one prick-eared look, then
scampers down the dusty creek.

A short-eared owl, freshly fallen
from last night's sky, is helpless
lying dead-wise across the road.

A raven circles, cracks her crooked beak
and waits for an echo from heaven.

I wish my best wish like always,
shift gears, and pull up
the Rye Creek hill, another option
that's left me still looking
for what I'll never find anyway.

THE SKIES OVER NEVADA

Whoever said you can't
learn by studying *nothing*
wasn't a philosopher
or a Nevadan.
In Nevada, nothing is
everything. We make do
with what we have—
even due north.

Most directions we travel
without. We've forgotten
how the constellations rotate
(things you probably think about
every day). Try as we do
tailing Hydra's too tough.
There's always dust
moving somewhere
and we have to check it out.

We know where we are
and there is plenty of room
to be here, too.
Consider the Humboldt Sink
bigger than the Copper Pit
(the world's largest Glory Hole)
or Esmeralda County
where a citizen can wander
bewildered all her life
looking for the Lost Dutchman.

When we lay our dreams
end to end, they don't reach
the horizon, and we've learned
to be content with just that
much less of everything.

THOUSAND SPRINGS, IDAHO: OUTLET FOR LOST RIVERS

When we walked to where all water is
    rewoven
to the river's loom that winds among
the finest fabric of loam
you knew as no one I had ever known
the hands that pass the shuttle are the
    shuttle,
the fabric is the thread
letting itself out of its own mouth
to join a patchwork of waves
tumbling dry in the sun.

In this water, bolts of bright color,
depth is woven with the woof,
light is woven with the warp,
eyes are unspun like yarn
beyond the reach of arm or mind.

So we went: blindly dancing
down the quilted creek bottom
ecstatic as fresh fish having
returned to dye the redd
with semen—the water foaming
with the white lint
of silk and monk's cloth.

A BELL MOUNTAIN FRAGMENT

Unlike your neighbor who lost her mind
trying to gather it up,
the mountain you see was never itself
always pieces of something else:
a sea floor for example
a canyon turned wrong side out
a prairie (the home of a single bee).

If you have time, wait
the mountain will move again
and when it does, church bells will ring
all over the world.

Remains

re·mains (rĭ-mānz) *pl.n.* **1.** All that is left after other parts have been taken away, used up, or destroyed. **2.** A corpse. **3.** The unpublished writings of a deceased author. **4.** Ancient ruins or fossils.

of

of (u v: *unstressed* əv) *prep.* **1.** Derived or coming from: originating at or from. **2.** Caused by: resulting from. **3.** Away from: at a distance from. **4.** So as to be separated or relieved from. **5.** From the total or group comprising. **6.** Composed or made from. **7.** Associated with or adhering to. **8.** Belonging or connected to. **9.** Possessing: having. **10.** Containing or carrying. **11.** Speciᵛed as: named or called. **12.** Centering upon (some object): directed toward. **13.** Produced by: issuing from. **14.** Characterized or identiᵛed by. **15.** Concerning: with reference to; about. **16.** Set aside for: taken up by. **17.** Before: until. Used in telling time. **18.** During or on (a speciᵛed time). **19.** *Rare.* By [Middle English *of*, Old English *of* (preposition and adverb.)]

Time

2

time (tīm) *n.* **1.** A nonspatial continuum in which events occur in apparently irreversible succession from the past through the present to the future. **2.** An interval separating two points on this continuum, measured essentially by selecting a regularly recurring event, such as the sunrise, and counting the number of its occurrences during the interval: duration. **3.** *Abbr.* A number, as of years, days, or minutes, representing such an interval. **4.** *Abbr.* A similar number representing a speciᵛc point, such as the present, as reckoned from an arbitrary past point on the continuum. **5.** A system by which such intervals are measured or such numbers are reckoned. **6.** *Often plural.* An interval marked by similar events, conditions, or phenomena: especially, a span of years: era. **7.** One's heyday. **8.** A suitable or opportune moment or season. **9.** A moment or period designated, as by custom, for a given activity. **10.** An appointed or fated moment, especially of death. **11.** One of several instances. **12.** An occasion. **13.** *Informal.* A prison sentence. **14.** The customary period of work. **15.** The rate of speed of a measured activity. **16.** The characteristic beat of musical rhythm. **1.** Simultaneously. **2.** At a period or moment in the past. —Out-of-date. —Temporarily. —Once in a while. —To run too fast. Said of a timepiece. —Long overdue. **1.** When or before due. **2.** Quickly. —Almost instantly. —**1.** Before the time limit expires. **2.** Within an indeᵛnite amount of passing time. —**1.** To make progress: proceed quickly. **2.** *Slang.* To make progress in pursuit of a girl's favors. —**1.** Promptly: according to schedule. **2.** By paying in installments. —*adj.* **1.** Of or relating to time. **2.** Constructed so as to operate at a particular moment. **3.** Payable on a future date or dates. **4.** Of or relating to installment buying. —*tr.v.* **timed, timing, times. 1.** To set the time for. **2.** To adjust to keep accurate time. **3.** To regulate for the orderly sequence of movements or events. **4.** To record the speed or duration of. **5.** To set or maintain the tempo, speed or duration of. [Middle English *time*, Old English, *tīma.*]

DIGGING

1)

We camp just off the dry creek bed
east of Albert Taylor's house,
roof fallen, furniture burned

by corporate cowboys
who write bad poetry
on Wrangler-brand laptops
and shoot coyotes that yip and yowl.

We drink brandy to Albert,
throw a log on the fire
and drink one more time
to his ghost.
He is here, somewhere, looking
for the table he sat at for a week
playing solitaire with Rigor Mortis.

Someone tells this story:
he got his power from the rock art
on the cliff above his cabin.
In return he offered cans of wildflowers
bundles of sticks, and spoke Paiute
when he was picking and preparing them.

He died sitting up—
just right for the pickup seat
he was hauled away on.

We drink again to Albert,
to his ghost, to rock art,
to the stars, to tomorrow's dig,
and turn ourselves in
to sleep off the restlessness.
Someone says sleep with your mouth closed
or your ghost will exercise all night
and tomorrow you will daydream
and we will never get you back
turned to wind like that.

2)

The trail to the rock-shelter follows
the creek bed whose water the cowboys
have stampeded upstream
and diverted to no better use.
The shelter is just a snuggle
under a cliff face.
We dig through the clamshell
through what we think is roof fall

and through the charcoal lens.
Sometimes a stone tool,
a rodent's skull, a femur is found.

There's talk of Eastgate,
side-notched and basal flaking.
There's more, but I am fixed
on the rattler climbing the juniper
behind us—and last night
as I walked toward my tent
my shadow sloughed off, and I am tender
under my new skin, nervous as a rabbit
caught in a net of stars,
speechless at last.

29

ANOTHER TIME

The grasses put out
every available root,
turning the soil to sod
so abruptly
the barn was caught
off balance.

Barb and hog-wire
snap,
slipping through staples
like anorexic wrists
sloughing handcuffs.

The barrel thrust
in the trampled ground
kept its toxic spill
(contained):
every drop of Penta,
diesel, and crankcase oil.

The fence posts were
as deranged as lunatics
loose at noon.

This is where
the world came to
a screaming halt
when there was no one
to listen.

But beyond
the distant horizon,
the one the near-sighted
have never seen,
the sky stretched overhead
and the center held

another time.

JUKEBOX CAVE

On an abandoned air force base near Wendover, Utah

There is no music now
unless you count the elegy
limestone sings inside itself
or the hum a cave makes.
But if you had a megaphone
made of time
and turned it toward history,
you might hear Glenn Miller
some moonlit night . . .
and you would be tempted
to pick a song on the jukebox
and sit wrapped around
a long-neck bottle of beer
and let the cool air
dance through your hair.
Another dozen beers
(who's counting the songs?)
and fatigue would open
like a parachute
and you would, finally,
start coming down
on a beach water abandoned
thousands of years ago.
And nothing time could do
would push you from your chair
so well-centered
the world would have to spin
around you.

IN HELLS CANYON

nothing a compass points toward
is possible to discover.

Turn around three times
then walk in any direction
you can still name, or
follow yourself by stepping
backwards around the circle
you just made, or
get out your map and find
the X where you think you are.
Identify this with something
already named, like
the Seven Devils or Lost Valley.

Study all the tracks you can find.
Notice game trails
never go in a straight line.
Notice the few trees
are rented out by the limb.
(Notice you have started
repeating yourself
the way you did in seminary,
as if by saying the same prayer
you'll find an answer,
as if by saying the same prayer
you'll have the sense
to recognize yourself—
if you get out of here.)

Sit cross-legged until the moon rises
then climb straight up.
Say nothing into the wind.
Words have a way of getting lost
in a place so simple
compasses don't even work.
And if you don't make it
no one will blame you.
Some people have been lost
in this place forever. . . .

THE CITY OF ROCKS

This is the city no one built.
Each monolith and boulder
is crafted by wind and water.
For convenience
all the streets run downhill
and disappear in the distance.

Right now, hawks are out
tag teaming your lunch.
Raven, Rabbit, and Coyote
are wandering wherever you go.
And the silence, the silence
is the sound of flowers:
purple-eyed mariposa,
penstemon, and paintbrush—
especially paintbrush
as it applies more color.

And all over town the sky is empty
except for one far-away cloud
idling above soft rain
hanging down.

If you get lost, just knock
and every door will open.

INSTRUCTIONS FOR A CEREMONY IN APRIL

When Sage and Sharp-tail strut
we must meet at the Booming Grounds
and lay out our bedrolls on dry grass
from where we will watch them dance
at dawn:

we will wait until a male begins
booming and night has sped from under us
like a windfall of falling stars
and the desert dancer has danced
over this ripe ground

and the shy hen has chosen
whether he and she will rendezvous.

RAILROAD CANYON AT SIXTY

One day you make a corner
and the road turns toward the sky.
The sky is not what you expect—
a lean blue—
but fat folds of violent gray.

On your right, cliffs
reams of endless history.
And here and there, a loose page.
Call it rock-shelter or cave.
It reads no better
than the Braille cobbles of the creek
you keep crossing.

The car pulses at sixty.
Road kills flatten into leather.
Leather into dust. Dust . . .
a long trailer you pull
behind your life.

Suddenly you remember an old trick:
double-clutching.
Your mood shifts smoothly.
The engine you know
better than your own heart labors
making lonely sounds of hollow
that drum under the hood.

This road is a canyon
so narrow only the dead
turn around without dying:
at sixty the car fishtails
and a prayer oscillates
between your helpless hands.

COLLECTING CAMAS

What could be a creek in better country
oozes its way among camas roots,
trickles through rock,
sinks out of sight and rises farther on.
It will never see the light
at the canyon's end
since it sinks for the last time
a quarter mile above that.

But what we have come for is
onion round and potato sweet
and care is spent digging down for bulbs.
With a pull and a twist, we wrench

them, finally, from spongy soil
that gives and giving yields
another camas.

We are one of the animals
gathering food
keeping our eyes peeled:
often we stop, camas root dangling
from our hand, and look
for what we cannot see but feel.
Then we bend back to dig
another camas.

When we stand, looking around
we see the future
more clearly than the world we live in
and for that we are content collecting
     camas.
So, when we walk out of the canyon
loaded like camels
our trip across the desert is
measured, not in the distance
we are from water
but by what we carry.

GIBSON-JACK

Could you fix yourself
and be changed
the way ice and water
alter by degree,
it would do for you
to do just that:

some afternoon
needle your way down
through warm threads of light
burning like a rainbow
among Doug fir
and take a slow look
into the creek where water
holds nothing back:

not your sadness
not the black pearls
your eyelids polish
with each tear they push,
not your rumpled hair
nor your face, rippled
in its own cold-hill-run.

You could come to this place
and put your shoulder against
the hard rock of misfortune
and work it round—
add one more turn
to a stone already true.

DIRECTIONS TO WILSON BUTTE

Take a finger and run it along
the straight edge of your imagination.
Now tie a plumb-line to the wind
and score the sky. Follow the course
it makes until you reach
the center of the world. You can't miss it.
It looks just like the desert itself:
creamy-white and autumn-warm,
plenty of lava and sage and prickly pear.
But if you do get lost, keep driving.
The roads out here go everywhere.
Eventually, you'll come back to yourself

the way the past returns to the future.
As you arrive, it will be the present
and that's where I'll be, keeping tumbleweeds
out of the cave's mouth, looking for a key
someone left under this or that stone
or watching sunset or dawn from the
     balcony
of the world, or resting in shadowy solitude
while old dreams are hefted away
by dust devils: mirages
in the summer heat
crossing a world of open space.

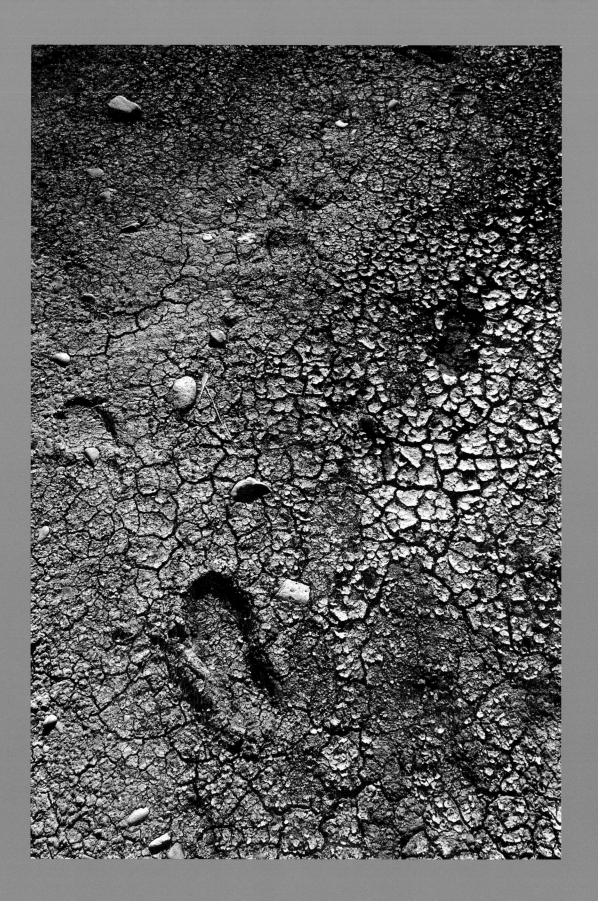

HONEYMOON IN OWYHEE

The birds are gutted and skinned
(cleaned as we say).
The dogs are fed and tied.
Potatoes are baking in the fire.
Coffee cooks on the coals.

We follow the moon
to the riverbank
where we take turns
soaping down with sand
until our chalk-white skin
glows pure as peeled apples.

Like the moon we will change shape
but tonight we will sleep
curled in a crescent
and all the stones in the desert
will be stars. . . .

NIGHTFIRE

1)

Gathering firewood by moonlight
each stick looks like a snake.
Some too much to risk. I pass them over
holding those crooked in my arm tighter.
The wood I find is old sage
a few willows washed upshore by storm
and roots without trees.

Loaded, I stop and look at the moon.
It is no one to me. I know its light
is false and uninhabitable.
So on trips like this
when the moon is full and the desert glows
and the Jerusalem crickets come close to
    camp,
I keep the fire banked.

2)

As I stoke the fire for the night
the flames flick the wind's lips
with orange fingertips.
Sparks dance into space, vanish.

The wood I use is
from the cradle of darkness.
I pick a piece, place it on the fire
where it hisses smoke
then flames, making a pocket
of living light like the sun.

THE WIND'S ECCLESIASTICAL HISTORY OF UTAH

1)

Before the Mormons came, there were just
   enough
Utes, Paiutes, traders, and trappers to keep
this place from getting lost.
I spent my time setting speed records
on the great salt flat
and shaping what I felt in stone.
Or I climbed the Wasatch Front
and tried to remember the first man I saw
come walking down the Corridor.

Sometimes I sat at his fire
or in the mouth of his cave or tent
and listened to his tales
of a godfather like the sun
of a godmother like the moon
of a world like an island in the sky.

2)

When the Mormons came crawling,
   pushing, pulling
across the prairie desert
herding their animals
driving their women and children
cracking the words of their prophets—
Lehi, Nephi, Moses, and Smith—
like a skinner's whip
over the heads of weary families,
I heard them clear from Illinois
as they put their shoulder to the wheel
and sang their way across the impossible.

They came to this odd land,
leftover like a dog's thumb, to live.
(It is peculiar . . . what a cripple sees
in the crippled:

this desert is a rose;
these pilgrims are saints.)
When they dropped to their knees
the desert caught them.
They planted prayers and children
side by side
and when the seeds grew
they took up the prayers and children
filling the storehouse of their Lord.

Sometimes I sat at their fire
or in the doorway of their temple
and listened to their tales
of a godfather like the sun
of a godmother like the moon
of a world like a star shining in the sky.

3)

There are nights I still talk to Big Wolf
and help with the deepest vowel of his voice.
There are mornings I keep for Moroni;
the sound of his name is a message
I have said for years.
There are days I wander around
(among my non-wives)
uttering the twelve languages of Babel:—

Every now and then there's a flurry for God;
someone rallies the banner—In These Latter
    Days—
but mostly it's peaceful: flags to flap,
clouds to carry, waves to wave, dust to dust.

You know—business as usual.

Practice

prac·tice (prăk´tĭs) *v.* **-ticed, -ticing, -tices.** — *tr.* **1.** To do or perform habitually or customarily: make a habit of. **2.** To exercise or perform repeatedly in order to acquire or polish a skill. **3.** To give lessons or repeated instructions to; drill. **4.** To work at, especially as a profession. **5.** To carry out in action: observe. **6.** *Obsolete.* To plot (something evil). —*intr.* **1.** To do or perform something habitually or repeatedly. **2.** To work at a profession. **3.** *Obsolete.* To intrigue or plot. Used with *against* or *with.* —*n.* Also **prac tise. 1.** A habitual or customary action or way of doing something. **2. a.** Repeated performance of an activity in order to learn or perfect a skill. **b.** *Archaic.* The skill so learned or perfected. **c.** The condition of being skilled through repeated exercise. **3.** The act or process of doing something: performance. **4.** The exercise of an occupation or profession. **5.** The business of a professional person. **6.** *Plural.* Habitual actions or acts that are objectionable, questionable, or unacceptable. **7.** The methods of procedure used in a court of law. **8.** *Archaic.* **a.** The act of tricking. **b.** A stratagem: trick. [Middle English *practisen,* from Old French *practiser, pratiquer,* from Medieval Latin *practicāre,* from Late Latin *practicus.*. PRACTICAL.]

§3

Range

range (rănj) *n. Abbr. Abbr.* r. **1. a.** The extent of perception, knowledge, experience, or ability. **b.** The area or sphere in which an activity takes place: scope. **c.** The full extent covered by something. **2. a.** An amount or extent of variation. **b.** *Music.* The gamut of tones within the capacity of a voice or instrument. **3. a.** The maximum or effective distance that can be traversed, as by bullets or by radiation. **b.** The distance to a target. **4.** The maximum distance that a ship or other vehicle can travel before exhausting its fuel supply. **5.** A place for shooting at targets. **6.** *Aerospace.* A testing area in which rockets and missiles are fired and flown. **7.** an extensive area of open land on which livestock wander and graze. **8.** The geographical region in which a kind of plant or animal normally lives or grows. **9.** The act of wandering or roaming over a large area. **10.** *Mathematics.* The totality of points in a set established by **mapping 11.** *Statistics.* A measure of dispersion equal to the difference in interval between the smallest and largest of a set of quantities. **12.** A class, rank, or order. **13.** An extended group or series, especially of mountains. **14.** One of a series of double-faced bookcases in a library stack room. **15.** A single series or row of townships, each six miles square, extending parallel to, or numbered east and west from, a survey base meridian line. **16.** A type of large cooking stove on which several foods may be cooked at the same time. —*v.* **ranged, ranging, ranges.** — **1.** To arrange or dispose in a particular order, especially in rows or lines. **2.** To assign to a particular category, classify. **3.** To align with a target: to train: to sight. **4. a.** To determine the distance of. **b.** To be capable of reaching. **5.** To move or travel over or through, as in exploration. **6.** To put on a range to graze. **7.** *Nautical.* To uncoil on deck so the anchor may descend easily. —*inf.* **1.** To vary within specified limits. **2.** To extend in a particular direction. **3.** To extend in the same direction. **4.** To move over or through a given area as in exploration. **5.** To roam or wander, rove. **6.** To live or grow within a particular region. [Middle English, series, line, from Old French *range, renge,* range, rank, from *renc, reng,* line, row, from Frankish *hring* (unattested), circle, ring.]

BASCO

In a country
he can't even speak
squat on his haunches
humped over a fire
he studies the ground.
What he sees is a woman.
She is stretched out
like the desert.
Her belly is flat and firm.
Her breasts rise
buttes in the distance.
Why they don't sink
and level off
like everything else

is the mystery
she always leaves
with her men.
He reaches out to touch.
Smiles to himself.
His hands
not empty or jilted
but warm and approved.
Tomorrow he will move
along her thigh
toward the Centennial Valley.
His sheep . . . uncertain
of how he guides them.

FOR YOUR PART

For the sake of setting things straight
let's say you pulled off the freeway
and stripped off your moral habit
untied your liberal politics
cashed in your economic recovery
gave up guilt and granola
opened the door on your closed marriage.

Let's say you parked for a long time
so long generations of grass grew
and mice dug bomb shelters under your tires.

Pack rats built nests
in your carburetor and for years
traded electrical wiring
for rat things—

Let's say you really didn't care.
The world you drove up in rusted
and you learned the secret of silence
and you let silence speak for itself
and took no credit for your part.

DRINKING FROM A CATTLE TROUGH

You do this because
it is the only water
because your tongue
has thickened from breathing
because the desert taunted you
and kicked heat down your throat
until you choked.

With both hands
you part the green scum.

You are no Moses
but the clear water below
is a miracle for which
you would risk everything.

Between drinks you watch
mosquito larvae
flip and jerk up and down.
Your last drink is quick
not as deep as the first.

TRACE ELEMENTS AROUND THE SAYLOR CREEK BOMBING RANGE

We accept the dilapidated cabin
as the end of the road,
park the truck, front wheels
turned toward the hillside,
rocks wedged tightly under tires—
an extra hitch
so she won't roll off while we're gone.

Beyond the cabin the rock corral,
the fence that keeps to the ground
as if the landscape might wander away,
a trail sputters in and out
of a dry creek bed
then staggers through a grove
of Rocky Mountain juniper

(the smell of gin . . . faint
among the flakes of parched snow).

As we duck under the trees
(limbs neck-high) a kingbird shrieks
and coyotes abandon their tracks
where the trail veers up
past small caves and rockshelters
where no one's been home
for five hundred years.

(What if we lived here? Turned the truck
loose from her tether at the end of the road?)

What if we lived here and this storm,
broken once by a bird's screech
and again by its wings
as flight feathers scuffed the cold air,

settled in and settling in
became all we know of next door
and all we want of grace?

The river . . . not far
a trip we'd take every day
and today we take it and stand on ripples
that leaped and never came down:
something of how time was
of how the world is the same:
earth, fire, wind, and water.

ABANDONING THE BODY

Geese call as they fly.
Their shadows fall behind them
sinking to the lake bottom.

A convoy of gulls lists past.
Li Po drifts by bobbing for the moon.
Voices of starlight sing to me.

My soul jumps its body-ship
and falls spinning in green space
toward a raft of coots walking
back and forth over the face of the lake.

My falling reflects off the water.
My shadow draws toward itself
death to a dying body.

Li Po's body rises to the surface.
His arms stretched out
hold the pale reflection of the moon,
a paper target against his chest.

Dead center.
I pass through his body
exchanging looks of surprise.

ENEMIES

I have come a long way
by headlight and memory
to this black basalt rim
high above the Bruneau
to listen as the sun warms up
turning subtle shades of sage
into silent gray
for tourists
and the disappointed.

At high noon
I will release a volume
of photos, enemies
and strangers who stood in
while shots were fired.
I will throw them
over the edge to fade
among kangaroo rats and scree.
I will fly backwards
(although the air is pitted
by 10,000 wingbeats)
and dance on the west wall
hairless and plump
as a young camas bulb Buddha.
I will not tell the tourists
I have thrown away my enemies
colored and black-and-white.
I will just listen

to the light padded feet
of late afternoon tapping out
my naked shadow among them.

BUTTE CITY, IDAHO NATIONAL LABORATORY, ACCELERATION, HALF-LIVES

The town, a wide spot
the highway doesn't slow down for
anymore, huddles under
a shell of lead oxide.
Every house is painted gray
with constant neglect.

But I tell my children this
is where a great physicist lived
unbending light
taking the curve out of gravity
so the semi-erect power poles
the abandoned buildings
the collapsed cars
and the Four Winds Bar
would seem, always, still
to be standing.

He painted merchandise
in the store window
with silver nitrate
and He, Himself, became
a hologram beveled in
a pane of lead glass
above the entrance to
Christ's First Community Church
and Resurrection Hall.

TERRA INCOGNITO

The map (*mappa mundi*) spreads out
as if it could be the world
as if a fingerprint could be the hand.

I dust it off, turn north north.

The line I'm on is marked *improved*
but my way has hardly been smooth.
I've had so many hard knocks
I can't keep up a frown.
I'm fatigued
faltering as I fumble—
all thumbs among map folds.

What I want is wilderness
a place the gods forgot
the Bureau of Land Management never
    found
where I can abandon my motor home
and no one will look for it—
where I can abandon all hope
and no one will find it.

What I want is a wilderness
where the sage is so thick
the grass can't be counted
and no one can enter except
through holes in the map
worn by rescuers
who gave up the search.

THE BIG-SKY MAP OF IDAHO

A mad Montanan made this map.
The last point of real reconnoiter,
the intersection of Highway 78 and Ruth,
was years ago. 78 petered out
in some-other-day's dusk, and Ruth,
the woman you kiss in your sleep,
has a subdivision named after her.

There are X's for
Crooked Creek, Asshole Springs,
Hell's Canyon, The Big Lost,
Clearwater, and Athol.
But the back roads to Ruth
are all chuckholes and canyons.
You keep an eye on the sky
where it falls
between two mountains over Ruth.

The only way to get even
is to feed the map
to the wind mile after mile
until there's so much dust
between you and her
nothing can ever be settled.

SALVATION AND THE BADLANDS RAPID

When the mudslide came sliding across the
    river
some folks said, "That's the end."
and started packing up, getting ready to go.
Some went, wouldn't wait for the water
to find its new level.

When they looked up
they thought they saw Bliss
coming down the hill.
That's how talk of damnation set in
and the Church of Christ got too hot
because people were praying so hard
the town broke out in a sweat.

Folks were confused: the hill had slumped
and slid, the town was undermined
and coming down, the church couldn't hold
all those who needed held.
Hell surely had a hand in this.

Then, as if a river could be moved
by prayer, the left bank cut loose
and boiled out the Badlands Rapid
where you can practice baptism
without anyone laying on a hand.

ON THE ROAD TO DEATH, NEVADA

At first the hills held their ground
as we moved motionless across
and across the same sagebrush flat.
Neither time nor speed changed
our location. But, abruptly, the hills
made their move and came up
on all sides of the car.
Scenery so quickly altered

couldn't find an end to itself:
small sagebrush flat, smaller meadow,
small sagebrush flat, smaller meadow.
We picked a hill to help mark progress.
That was as close as we got.
It drifted back and forth above the road
as if confused by such importance,
fleeing, finally, far to the north.

Five hours of the same strange landscape
of the same one-piece sky
of the same narrow-gauge, dirt road . . .

We repeated our conversations,
ate sandwiches, drank pop and Perrier
until nothing was left but fragments
and wrappers and empty containers.
We made wax paper targets, shot holes
in Coke cans, and talked incoherently—
the way people do whose lives
are pitted from gravel and fine dust.

I want to say that there was more:
we taught the children to drive,
we slept with the windows down,
we tried to make a life of it.
But each time we got out, we were
in the same place, never closer.
We went on anyway, knowing
Death, Nevada, would

just, suddenly, be there.

ALTERING THE FLOW

At the Malad Gorge
you can look straight down
and never stop getting dizzy
the way water makes a stream
of itself all swirls and froth
falling foamy in so much air—
too thin for fish to live in.
The bank is an idea that never happened,
no room between boulder and cliff.
This water is mad for itself
and would be free
except for sins of omission: